SNOWFIRE AND HOME

ALEXANDER ETHERIDGE

T0303646

POEMS

Fort Smith, Arkansas

Snowfire and Home

Versions of some of these poems were published previously:
Susurrus: "Find the Earth"
Abridged: "Living Will"
The Madrigal: "Letter to Her"
Forge Zine: "Second Season Wish"
Welter Journal: "White Elk"
Museum of Americana: "On the Prairie"
Riddled With Arrows: "Writing in a Flood"

Cover image: Alexander Etheridge

Edited by Casie Dodd
Design & typography by Belle Point Press

Belle Point Press, LLC
Fort Smith, Arkansas
bellepointpress.com
editor@bellepointpress.com

Find Belle Point Press
on Facebook, Substack,
and Instagram (@bellepointpress)

Printed in the United States of America

28 27 26 25 24   1 2 3 4 5

ISBN: 978-1-960215-11-6

CHAP9/BPP21

Contents

Writing in a Flood

All the slight degrees of dark
prove nothing's simple, like thoughts after
zero was imagined. *Shadowhood and*
rain
post–temporal seas

You only enter the otherworld alone.

I look for water the way it was
before it was ever seen, but this is more words

and it's getting late.
Who said *grim currents*
of the riptide

who said *undertow*
A page is an opened light before the words
darken it. If I say it out loud,
I'm already under water.

Dream of Two Memories

Think back to the tree-huddle,
dad was there and the cicadas sounded like
rust. The elm light was watery.

Flatland rail-line
blueish at dark and leading out
to a dark earth. Earth also recalls.

Remember that handful of
luminous yellows
in a late April
storm.
You waited at the foot of the mind's ladder.

Sound of the sparrow flocks
echoing,
and a blue gloomy cloud-cover.

You're eight and you stumble through cloudfall.
Years later lined up at the
empty pulpit,
you brought the wrong key
and a black thread was spun.

Night after night, a rush of
smoke—that entire life is gone.
Gone is the first thing you remember.

Continuum

Thunder-welts
rattle a lush of wickerbranches
outside my window—
drifts of ashy stars
over lakes and burials,
Heaven's faces
closed over with light, mud tracks of horseback armies
mirrored in a bead,
candles,
turns of smoke in
choir lofts.
A fire going out.
A fire lit.

One sustenance—
each time the echo sends the voice back up.

Two poles and a white connective heat . . .

Faces in a photograph
changing at the speed of trains.

Tracked into breezes by wildfire,
figures wilting in petal smoke,
delicate as onion feathers.
Incineration and a next world, flowers
light as glances . . . fire-lifted,
the flowers change.
Earth written by scent
and ash, then falling from sense
to come up in our eyes another day.

Last Change of Address

The earth knows we'll return—
our few feeble movements
down under the flowers,
and our names repeated like a song's chorus
so the ones left won't forget
through all the winters.

Look,
moon, sun, and moon and sun again,
the mist coming down
to the cold lake and the churchyard—
It'll all be forgotten.

The Bloodstone

A green rocky creek runs beside it,
the ancient stone with something like
the face of a man, its strange features
of brutal centuries—Ice and fire, slow nights

under a witches' moon. You can see it all
turning in the stone's deep geographies—
Rugged paths through a forest, snakes under
an ocean, crow-calls echoing in a huge valley

at twilight. The stone cracks but never
moves, as if it grew powerful roots down
into the cellar of the earth. The stone forgets
nothing, and its dreams become your own.

Follow the Earth

   We're led by a billowing fog
down the footpath to where the copse goes dark.
We unwind the thread
made of stems and black snowcrystals.
(. . . hands drifting high over sycamores, teeth
in mineral crush)

Stepping over ages of sediment, we find the beech trees
and the elms,
the briars and the frost—

the morning hours of winter,
before we're called into dirt.

In the Storm

Ruin of nightfall
The world's relic of iced-over ponds
and clipped light

The voice you hear in the empty house
is your own—
   earth, where the winter has begun

The garden is freezing
Snow-gusts through black petals

Blizzard
blowing in through the open door

Midnight's foot-tracks
and plunged
stars

The Door
—for Olav H. Hauge

It's October here
where second by second
I lose the entire
world, and gain it back again.
Is this the way it was
meant to be—such gifts
and such grief?

While I sit and stare,
the cottonwoods
all around me keep their
wings up
over red and delicate
wild berries, rust-colored
brambles, and scattered lemon leaves.
The heart of the earth

is untroubled and calm
like a hidden pond
between nightbreezes.
I want the words

that will give me up to
the silent mind of
autumn, maybe one word,
my last thought

like a door opening

into the cool orchards
I dreamt of long ago.

Night's Valley

There's fire, then later on,
antifire—I don't know how else
to describe it, the way snow
falls into the mind.
I don't know where I am

anymore, and all the roads
are buried in ash.
Blindness now

is seeing. There's a trail I dreamt of

where light collapses.
Being lost everywhere is
home—life, then antilife,
out here

under dark and dazzled stars.

Inside a Picture of Trees

   Aster vines between the trunks
Sunlight
cross-clipped by limb shadows

December
and a line of oaks burned stark by the cold

The yellowberry and nettle
share the grave of the poplar

Our world
is long alone

Bloodfire

Quiet rover and winter endurer,
climbing snowy hills, rising into purple
cloudfall—Kory Bloodfire, following
the footfalls of sunset. Come back when you can
down the stoney path, through
shredding hail, to the other side of night—
Kory, the dark is burning, and your prayers
vanish into January earth
there where the aspens and the poplars
turn grim in a blue forest afterglow.
The cold is churning, your sight is dim.
Follow the creek out of the brambles and thorns
through a clearing where the raven
calls to the lamb, down to the valley of the half-moon.
Return before the ground takes your home
and your children, your blonde wheat fields
and your lemon orchard, back into its bed
of damp clay and black tangled roots.

Address

Strange being here, strange *thinking* it,
stopped at the cold-gusted street
on an obscure planet along the edge of
a great emptiness.

The earth is bite-sized.
Cool salty oceans, spicy leaves,
rock and swampland—winter
and landslide, rusted gutter grills,
highway signs—
a lost herd of moviegoers in the abject city
with its trauma clouds and locked doors . . .

Crows crowding the sun.
Strange how words define us. *sun*
infinity vaporous

Huge stormcloud of crows. Our next home
is in the dark beyond stars.

World Alone

Of white marble—white seas
turned by the halo wind.

Be here where God is not.

It's all been given up—office towers and grain silos,
libraries and telescopes . . . a stairwell leading down
into the grave. Everything's lost
in the rubble of continents.

The thread runs bare when the dawn comes.
Be here.

Of massive craters in the ocean floor.

Of snowdrifts and cathedral dust,
the illegible voicelessness—

There's an open window in the empty
hospital, and tracks leading out into the stones.

And each thing everywhere
is left to its own
great solitude.

Living Will

We go on,
the blind lives,
dusting for prints. The center is everywhere,
the atmospheres smell like a great fire.
We kept a prayer book of paper cuts.
Our walk to the killing floor—a caught breath
of praise.
A fire going out.
Note on our mirror with a map
leading through trap doors. Hail five thousand years
of cell mates, family plots
and pottery dust.
The library of Eden
willed to a blizzard of relapsing fever.
Rubble-glass and hacking cough, timeline
of higher thought
like a series of bad dreams . . .
March all morning through dark

while storms raid the sea.
Hail Wintertide. Relic of whispers,
one word, maybe one
crossing over.

Second Season Wish

I tell you my head floats out in front of me
like a little moon, replacing itself
rapidly—a stroboscopic blink, like slag rakes flashing
the brutal mud
of melted iron.

My bones migrate inside me—
I watch them through a telescope.
My rib is a bare landmass, my eye,
a rock with propellers, making an arc
through big clouds of gearshifts and crows.

I bring only a syllable to the tables—
Sudden dusk wheels a pendulum crescent.

I tell you my hip is a monolith
grinding down into the mineshafts.
I say the dawn sun is pulled up by a thread.

And I set out from the word, climbing through
the windows of its two thousand rooms.
I leave myself to the summers . . .

I leave myself. I wish
the great open summers.

Prayer to the Muse

Out of the rough instant,
the second, the age,

   rain in black elms
   rain in the oaks, mist

   of the high crowns

you find me
one flash ahead of my ear.

   Solomon, Soren
   Bloodfire, Persephone

Find me, Queen of Birds,
in rings of grief,
in the illegible hour,

blind and abject without you.

White Elk

—for my grandmother

Listener of windy creeks, she leads her young
through the wind-frosted and desolate steppes—
Love is a furnace in her hooves.
Half frozen, she'd lie flat
with hail piling up, so the strays
could follow her pulse back.
Snowy elk, recalling again when
she heard a greenwood note
like little children sounding out names.
Now coming to her end, she thinks of her first calf
born on white and transparent leaves,
and with a cloudward
glance, sees an ancient promise begin to prove itself.

Note Left on Her Door

Winter dark—a path through frost and
bare thickets, down to the footsteps

of daybreak, where the sun
comes up beside an old bell tower. Follow the wind
    and the light

into the orchard, and open your eyes
unto me

Letter to Her

It's you translating the earth
　　into Nirvana—

　　september scale and alphabet

It's the ribbon
and white aster stems
in your hair

　　hands at rest　　an absolution
　　of mirror and root

Your name means snow
on the pomegranate

　　amnesty of sight

It's your hand in the drifting sycamores
Your name means

sleeper in the young wheat—field after field
learning the morning

And when alone we ask for you

Little kingfishers
carry the thread of your breathing

To Your Departure

You called your fires in through my open window.
The room was made hushed and spellbound
for the sacrament of the heat—
Blue petals in a furnace, lightning
in a church. And then you were gone.

This is the black ashes, architecture
of blaze and abyss. Riddle of your scarlets—

White indecipherable dusk and dawn. I see

big chains hung from the tree arches, winter ponds.
I watch daylight retreat along the borders
of an infinity. I've learned

that you do not return.

Pictures of Abigail

Empress of the Psalms
I learn your open eyes

By milk riddle and glance you startle
a listening of the cedars, ravens
over the sand
and we know that you've come

I send my asking up to you

Summer in the ruins
and smoke in the salt wells
June's drought
burns the black honeycombs

But through the marrow and thorns
a crawl tunnel leads out
to sapphire light

*

   Your high windows watch the hundred lakes
Little bells

follow the mouth of the sunrise
There's a trail up to the tower
and great open cypresses
ranged by the sugar fields

   You gaze the apricots
girl of the minor key, candle eye
beneath the forest arches

And the streams bring their word to the white
    of your hand

   Even I know this
   a roving shade far from the tower

Into the Trees

Masters of patience,
the endurers, with windy
hidden eyes.
Keepers of black frost and burning gales,
their long lives
spent learning earth's extremes—
the rime ice of December, or their ranks wasted
by tides of fire.

I've come a long way to join them here,
through years of nightmares and coma beds,
black dawns and blank pages.
From out of the long dusk
I walk over tangles of their ancient roots.
I've come to learn their question—
through deep blue and pale
yellow, their question is silence.

Under forest roofs I strip down my prayer.
Never alone here, may we never
be alone. All my wishes
come from the first wish.
In the kingdom of cottonwoods, willows, and oaks,
I'm listening to the tiny green highways of leaves.
I've walked here from the other side of twilight
to an ancient world, the keep of the trees.

.

On the Prairie

Blood on the saddle,
sky black, Hell red
here on the prairie.

Blood in your eye, this night
goes on and on. Dark light blazes up

in purgatorial orange.
Tonight you'll live through another blizzard.
The hardest part is knowing
you'll survive.

Cold deepens in
black wildflowers and wild
purple grass.

Blood meridian. At dawn
your world will fall further
into dark. At dawn

hailstones fly—

Your dream speaks with mouths
of dead flowers. Come home,
they say, come back
to unending cold,
and ghosts

along icy trails . . . your eyes watching

from the bad dream they were born into.
This home

where you'll meet yourself
as you once were,
and will be

again—
alone on the prairie.

Shepherd

Flock

Shepherd of slow granite

all night your flock of stars
rove over dark houses

and empty roads

Name

Shepherd of ancient glass
glinting in dusklight

Wanderer in fields of your
otherlife memory

It was scar tissue and
fire that unspelled your name

the day you were
born the day you

died
Now your silence stretches

into everything

Eternity

Nomad of snow
hail and freezing rain
the night you died you

led your wayward flock
over black hills and apple trees
as you were born

into another mind

on a path of its own
never-dying

its own forever

Appetite

Yours is the cycle of
desire and loneliness
Yet your stars

never know hunger
as they wheel through God's
great shadow

Your endless stars
follow you anywhere
sentinels

of a perishing world

Heaven

Old listener
bring your herd of blue-white fires

back into warm skies
over a wintery people
out there in lonely paradise

of nothing left
too late and
always gone

Valley

Constant walker
with one prayer left
there's an October creek
running by orchards

leading away through its thicket

of dreams

to the half-moon valley where your stars
sleep at last

Letting Flowers Go

I stood up at last and took a step into another
world—I walked for a hundred years and flew up
into a memory, the shadowy vision
of a desert valley, every inch
dry as a thistle blossom. I fell and I fell
again, there in someone else's life,
remembering with another man's mind
a dark chapel in sudden nightfall.

In my only life the skies crumble upward,
falling into black matter, and everything
carries the scent of ancient graves. All I see are
ways to peril, paths to that silence just before
a great explosion. In our lives there's only one
question—a wordlessness, the ladder to a throne
of stars. All we need to know
are cherry blossoms and sweet white-fire dusk.

We want to learn how to walk away,
how to let go, let the moon cinder,
let everything we love turn into snow. We're alone
with each other, all of us alone, with a scent
of orchard blossoms breezing in through the open
doors—we've been quiet and still, waiting
for so long. But our time is beautiful, as we've learned
watching it go, go back into the cool night.

ALEXANDER ETHERIDGE has been developing his poems
and translations since 1998. His poems have been featured
in *The Potomac Review, Scissors and Spackle, Ink Sac, Cerasus Journal,
The Cafe Review, The Madrigal, Abridged Magazine, Susurrus Magazine,
The Journal, Roi Faineant Press,* and many others. He was the
winner of the Struck Match Poetry Prize in 1999, and a
finalist for the *Kingdoms in the Wild* Poetry Prize in 2022. He
is the author of *God Said Fire*.